## My First Science Books
### A CRABTREE SEEDLINGS BOOK

# I Hear SOUND

**Francis Spencer**

CRABTREE
PUBLISHING COMPANY
WWW.CRABTREEBOOKS.COM

Listen! You are using your ears to hear.

Hearing is one of our five **senses**.

We use our **senses** to learn about our world.

# The **5** Senses:

**seeing**

**touching**

**hearing**

**smelling**

**tasting**

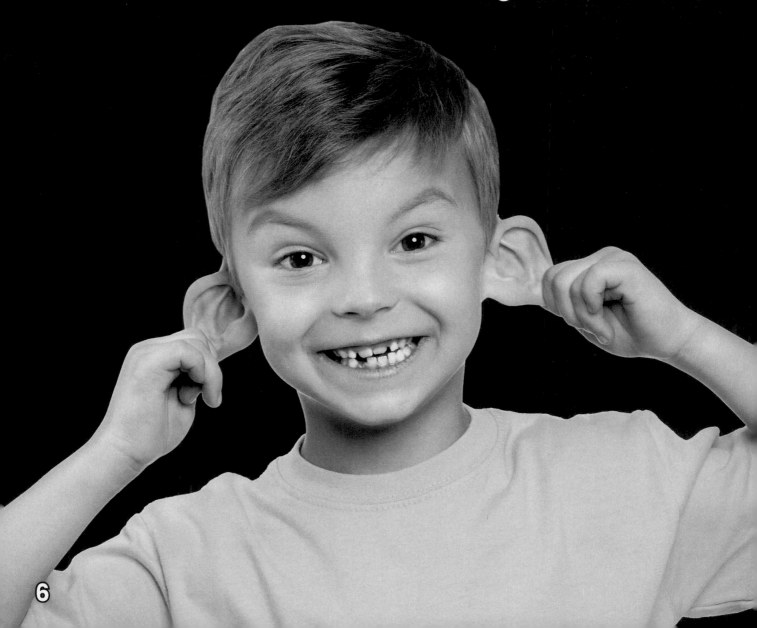

We have two ears for hearing.

# AMAZING ANIMAL EARS!

Caracals have tufts of hair on their ears. Scientists think the tufts may help them hear better.

A barn owl can hear a mouse on the soft forest floor 75 feet (23 meters) away.

Dogs can hear four times better than humans. They hear sounds that are impossible for humans to hear.

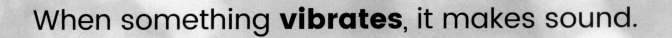

When something **vibrates**, it makes sound.

Pluck a guitar string. You can hear, see, and feel it vibrate.

Very fast **vibrations** have a high pitch.
Slower vibrations have a lower pitch.

Bees make a low buzzing sound
when they flap their wings.

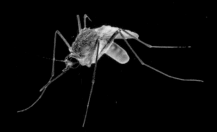

Mosquitoes flap faster.
Their wings make a higher
buzzing sound.

# Size can also affect pitch.

A large bell has a lower pitch than a smaller bell.

Vibrations make **sound waves**.
Sound waves can travel through air,
water, and **solids**.

This is a drawing of a sound wave.

A bird makes sound waves when it sings. They come from vibrations in its throat. Put your fingers on your throat and talk. Can you feel vibrations? When you talk, you are making sound waves!

sound waves

Sound waves go into your ear. They hit your eardrum and make it vibrate.

# This sends vibrations to a set of **nerves**.

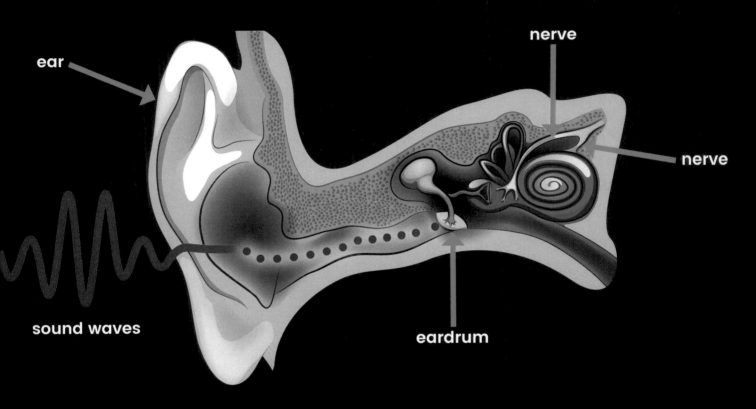

ear

nerve

nerve

sound waves

eardrum

The nerves send messages to your brain. Your brain uses the messages to tell you what sounds you are hearing.

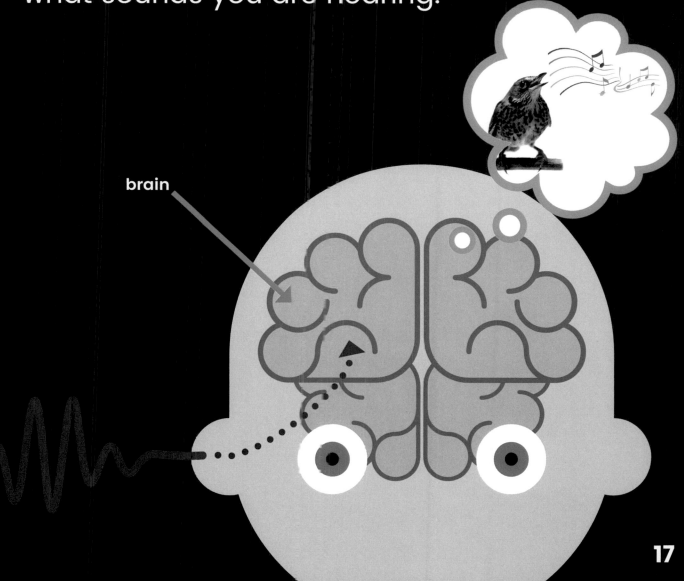

brain

# EXPERIMENT: MAKE A TELEPHONE

## Ask a grown-up to help you.

1. Find two clean, empty cans.

2. Use a hammer to drive a nail through the bottom of each can to make a hole.

3. Cut some string about 10 feet (3 meters) long.

4. Thread one end of the string through the bottom of each can and knot it so it stays.

5. Give one can to a friend, you hold the other.

6. Walk slowly apart until the string is tight.

7. Talk into your can. Can your friend hear you?

# Helpful Tools

There are tools we use with our ears:

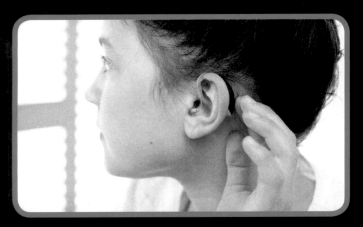

Hearing aids are tools that help people who cannot hear well.

Earbuds let you listen to sounds by yourself.

A speaker makes sounds louder.

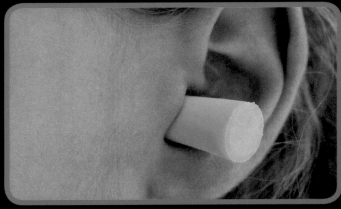

Earplugs protect ears from very loud sounds.

# What Did You Learn?

Read each question, then choose an answer. Find a sentence in the book that proves your answer.

1. **What makes sound?**

   vibrations        ears        nerves

2. **Which bell has the highest pitch?**

   **a.**         **b.**         **c.**

3. **What would be a useful tool at a loud rock concert? Why?**

   earplugs        earbuds        hearing aid

# Glossary

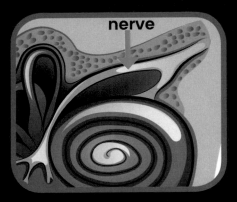

nerve

**nerves** (NURVZ):
Nerves are thin fibers
in your body that send
messages to your brain.

**senses** (SENSS-ez): Senses are the
five powers we use to help us enjoy
and stay safe in our world: touching,
seeing, tasting, smelling, hearing.

**solids** (SOL-idz): Solids
are hard or firm—not runny
like liquids. Ice is a solid.

**sound waves** (SOUND WAYVZ): Sound
waves are vibrations that move through
air, water, or solids, and can be heard
when they enter ears.

**vibrates** (VYE-braytes):
When something vibrates, it moves back and forth very quickly. A guitar string vibrates when you pluck it.

**vibrations** (VYE-bray-shuhnz):
Vibrations are fast back-and-forth movements. The fast wing movements of bees create vibrations that sound like buzzing.

## Index

# School-to-Home Support for Caregivers and Teachers

Crabtree Seedlings books help children grow by letting them practice reading. Here are a few guiding questions to help the reader with building his or her comprehension skills. Possible answers are included.

## Before Reading

- What do I think this book is about? I think this book is about how people hear sound.

- What do I want to learn about this topic? I want to learn about the different parts of the ear.

## During Reading

- I wonder why... I wonder why dogs have much better hearing than humans.

- What have I learned so far? I have learned that nerves and the eardrum are parts of the ear.

## After Reading

- What details did I learn about this topic? I learned that vibrations make sounds. Sounds travel to our ears in waves.

- Read the book again and look for the vocabulary words. I see the word *vibrates* on page 8 and the word *nerves* on page 16. The other vocabulary words are found on pages 22 and 23.

## Library and Archives Canada Cataloguing in Publication

Title: I hear sound / Francis Spencer.
Names: Spencer, Francis, 1973- author.
Description: Series statement: My first science books | "A Crabtree seedlings book". | Includes index. | Previously published in electronic format by Blue Door Education in 2020.
Identifiers: Canadiana 20200389637 |
  ISBN 9781427130242 (hardcover) |
  ISBN 9781427130358 (softcover)
Subjects: LCSH: Hearing—Juvenile literature. | LCSH: Sound—Juvenile literature. | LCSH: Ear—Juvenile literature.
Classification: LCC QP462.2 .S64 2021 | DDC j612.8/5—dc23

## Library of Congress Cataloging-in-Publication Data

Names: Spencer, Francis, 1973- author.
Title: I hear sound / Francis Spencer.
Description: New York, NY : Crabtree Publishing Company, 2021. | Series: My first science books ; a Crabtree seedlings book | Includes index.
Identifiers: LCCN 2020051006 |
  ISBN 9781427130242 (hardcover) |
  ISBN 9781427130358 (paperback)
Subjects: LCSH: Hearing--Juvenile literature. | Sound--Juvenile literature.
Classification: LCC QP462.2 .S66 2021 | DDC 612.8/5--dc23
LC record available at https://lccn.loc.gov/2020051006

## Crabtree Publishing Company

www.crabtreebooks.com          1–800–387–7650

e-book ISBN 9781427142504
e-pub ISBN  9781427142511

© 2021 Blue Door Education

**Author:** Francis Spencer

**Production coordinator and Prepress technician:** Tammy McGarr

**Print coordinator:** Katherine Berti

Printed in Canada/022022/CPC20220214

Photo credits: Cover © Robert Kneschke; page 4-5 © By Vlasov Volodymyr; page 6-7 illustrations © Gorbachev Oleg, kid with speech bubble © Rawpixel.com; page 8 © DenisNata, page 9 caracal © Stuart G Porter, barn owl © duangnapa_b, dog By Eileen Kumpf; pages 10-11 © Zurijeta; page 12 bee © irin-k, mosquito © Somboon Bunproy; page 14 © Alexander Weingart, page 15 © Robert Kneschke; page 16-17 © Kasefoto, sound waves © Telman Bagirov; bird page 16 and 18 © Rosa Jay, music notes © vectorgirl; page 18 © Artemida-psy, page 19 © MSSA, thought bubble thought bubble © akiradesigns; page 20: hearing aid © Robert Przybysz, boy at computer © Monkey Business Images, speakers © Yanawut Suntornkij, ear plug © Victoria 1; page 22 ice © Valentyn Volkov All images from Shutterstock.com

**Published in Canada**
Crabtree Publishing
616 Welland Ave.
St. Catharines, Ontario
L2M 5V6

**Published in the United States**
Crabtree Publishing
347 Fifth Ave.
Suite 1402-145
New York, NY 10016

**Published in the United Kingdom**
Crabtree Publishing
Maritime House
Basin Road North, Hove
BN41 1WR

**Published in Australia**
Crabtree Publishing
Unit 3 – 5 Currumbin Court
Capalaba
QLD 4157